ROYAL TEAS

Seasonal recipes from Buckingham Palace

MARK FLANAGAN

AND

KATHRYN CUTHBERTSON

ROYAL COLLECTION TRUST

CONTENTS

INTRODUCTION

ROYAL TEAS

> "There are few hours in life more agreeable than the hour dedicated to the ceremony known as *afternoon tea.*"

Henry James, *The Portrait of A Lady*, 1881

Tea is the quintessential British meal, from the springtime picnic to the 'high tea' of autumn afternoons. It is also a meal with impeccable royal connections: the woman credited with having created the concept of 'afternoon tea' was Anna Maria Russell, Duchess of Bedford (1783–1857), who served Queen Victoria as Lady of the Bedchamber from 1837 to 1841. By the mid-1840s dinner was being served later and later in the day in aristocratic circles, whilst lunch was often very light – leaving a long and hungry afternoon. Whilst visiting the 5th Duke of Rutland, the Duchess introduced the idea of afternoon tea to the Duke and his circle. It very quickly became popular in households of all classes. By 1861, in her *Book of Household Management*, Mrs Beeton could include lists of dishes and recipes suitable for 'high tea', 'family tea' and an 'at-home' tea.

Tea itself, as a drink, was introduced into England via the London coffee houses of the 17th century. Samuel Pepys first tasted it in 1660; Catherine of Braganza, Portuguese wife to King Charles II, brought the custom of tea-drinking with her from the Lisbon court, further popularising it. At this date, all the tea consumed in Europe was China tea, almost always drunk without milk and sometimes from the saucer, rather than the teacup or bowl. It was only in the nineteenth century that the British succeeded in cultivating the plant on large plantations in Assam in India and cheaper, more robustly flavoured Indian tea came to be the staple that it is today. The teapot and the tea plate reached the British tea table almost simultaneously.

Many of the dishes that are our teatime favourites today date back to the 19th century. The oldest-known recipe for carrot cake, for example, is to be found in a Swiss recipe book of 1892, whilst kedgeree, originally a breakfast dish, came from the Indian kitchens of the Raj. Victoria Sponge was of course named in honour of Queen Victoria, but all attempts to locate

Right: An Easter tea table – spring flowers, Simnel Cake and Hot Cross Buns.

Above: Springtime cordials in the summer house at Buckingham Palace; and a picnic in the garden (see recipe on page 21).
Opposite: Two pages from Mildred Nicholls' 'Recipe Book', now kept in the Royal Archives at Windsor Castle.
RA VIC/ADDC31

a particular 'Madeleine' to whom the invention of that particular treat might be credited have so far proved fruitless, although it is known that they were popular in France in the mid-18th century. The first printed recipe for shortbread appeared in Scotland at about the same time.

Others are far, far earlier. We were eating drop scones and crumpets (and presumably wiping butter off our chins) in medieval England. Mince pies, which originally contained a typically Mediterranean combination of real minced meat with fruits and spices, were brought back to England by knights returning from the Crusades at the end of the 14th century. Simnel cake is just as time-honoured, while the first recipes for crème brûlée, or 'burnt cream', date back to the mid-17th century.

Unsurprisingly, the royal garden parties at Buckingham Palace have a tradition of serving the teatime classics – dainty cucumber sandwiches, exquisitely scaled-down cakes and pastries, and, of course, tea. The garden parties became an institution in the reign of Queen Victoria, following celebrations for first her Golden then her Diamond Jubilee. Today over 30,000 guests attend the garden parties every year, consuming 27,000 cups of tea, 20,000 sandwiches and some 20,000 slices of cake.

Receipes

Mildred. D. Nicholls

Pastry

Buckingham Palace.

London.

Pouding Soufflé à la. Royale.

Cold Genoise Souffle au Citron. Apricot Sauce

Make Genoise in ordinary way with exception of Baking Powder. 1 lb is sufficient for 4 Baking Sheets. When just beginning to set. take out of oven, spread with Black or Red currant jelly & roll. When cold cut into thin Slices & stick round a well Buttered Souffle Mould. fill up with Souffle & Bake in Bain Marie in oven for 30 to 45 Minutes. Slow oven to start. Serve with apricot Sauce or Raspberries p.cc flavored with a little Vanila

In fact our teatime favourites have changed very little over the last hundred years or more. The Royal Library at Windsor Castle contains as one of its many treasures a handwritten recipe book compiled by a Miss Mildred Nicholls, who joined the Royal Household as 'Seventh Kitchen Maid' in 1908. Mildred conscientiously noted down recipes for a number of the dishes she helped prepare in the years before she left the household to get married in 1919, and many of them, such as 'HM The Queen's recipe for Bath Buns' would not look out of place on a tea table today. We still follow the tradition that savoury precedes sweet, and that the wholesome is to be consumed before the indulgent, but that the perfect tea table has to include a combination of both. In colder months, when sustenance of the more solid sort is needed, and the word 'teatime' conjures up visions of toasting crumpets at the fireside, before slathering them with butter and fragrant quince cheese, the sandwiches and cakes may be supplemented by sausage rolls, pâtes, and perhaps even a baked ham. This is the type of meal often referred to as 'high tea'.

Opposite: Dressed Asparagus (see recipe on page 18).

There is something both traditional and delightfully nostalgic in the idea of a proper afternoon tea. Perhaps our fondness for it comes from the fact that it reminds us of childhood. The unbreakable miniature tea service still lives in many a toy box, and favourite dolls and teddies may still be invited to tea if they behave themselves; while teatime treats such as sandwiches and sausage rolls, biscuits and slices of cake come in small sizes, suitable for little hands, and retain that charm even in their grown-up and more sophisticated versions. Silver cake forks and delicate doilies, pretty tea plates and embroidered tea cloths all seem to speak of a world that was both more leisurely and less complicated. One should make time for tea.

Undoubtedly the resurgence in popularity of teatime today has arrived hand-in-hand with a renewed interest in the art of baking. Sifting and sieving, folding and kneading have become skills every cook wishes to master. Rather than the latest high-tech slicer and dicer, today in our kitchens we are reaching again for the pudding bowl and the rolling pin. However, the recipes in this book are selected to be within the reach of any cook, whether experienced or not, as afternoon tea should always be a relaxed and enjoyable occasion. Or, as Emily Post, that doyenne of all things right and proper in social and domestic etiquette, would write in 1922, 'a tea, even though it be formal, is nevertheless friendly and inviting'.

The recipes in this book also showcase the best of the British summer, in berries and jams, and warm and comfort us in winter with ingredients from the woods and fields. There is always an emphasis in the entertaining at Buckingham Palace on using seasonal produce. The sequence of recipes in *Royal Teas* reflects this, and is also organised by season. Beyond that, however, to quote Emily Post again, 'the selection of afternoon tea-food is entirely a matter of whim'. In other words, we all have our favourites, with traditional recipes that are often handed on from one generation and one tea table to another. As an example, we might point to a recipe known in the royal kitchens as 'Her Majesty's Recipe for Drop Scones', from fifty years ago, which is traditionally said to have been sent by Queen Elizabeth II to President Eisenhower, and which is given on page 14.

While afternoon tea is clearly a custom that Britain has exported around the world, ingredients and weights and measures vary from country to country. All the recipes in this book are authentic to the kitchens at Buckingham Palace, but Mark Flanagan, the Royal Chef, has chosen them with an eye to ensuring that their ingredients are readily available and as easy to source as possible. Every recipe includes weights in US cups and spoons, as well as in grams. This book also includes a conversion table to negotiate your way more generally between UK and US weights and measures, and oven temperatures.

Her Majesty's Recipe for Drop Scones, *c*.1960

This type of small pancake, dropped on to a hot griddle to cook, has a place in almost every cuisine in the world. The drop scone, or 'Scotch pancake' is very similar to American breakfast pancakes, and can be eaten with melted butter, spread with jam, or served with maple syrup – all are equally good!

1 free-range egg
2 tablespoons unrefined caster sugar
1 teaspoon unsalted butter, melted
250ml (1 cup) full-fat milk
1 teaspoon bicarbonate of soda
240g (1⅞ cups) plain flour
2.5 teaspoons baking powder
1.5 teaspoons cream of tartar
(in the US you can substitute baking powder for both this and the bicarbonate of soda)
100g (½ cup) clarified unsalted butter

Equipment:
pancake griddle, or non-stick frying pan

1 In a mixing bowl sieve together the dry ingredients: flour, bicarbonate of soda, cream of tartar and sugar. Add to this the milk and egg and whisk to a smooth batter, finally adding the warm melted butter. Pass through a sieve to get rid of any lumps and if necessary thin with more milk. The batter should have a dropping consistency, but remain thick enough to retain its shape on the griddle.

2 Heat the griddle (or frying pan) over a medium heat and grease with clarified butter. Using a dessert spoon or small ladle, carefully pour spoonfuls of the batter on to the griddle. After one side has cooked, flip the scones with a palette knife to cook the other. Once you feel more confident you can cook a few scones at a time, being careful not to let them over-cook on either side.

3 Serve warm with butter and home-made preserves.

SPRING

Dressed Asparagus with Sauce Gribiche

The royal kitchens always try to use natural, local ingredients, tailoring menus to follow the seasons. In spring this means young green asparagus served with a simple sauce to complement the subtle flavour of the elegant, delicate spears.

20 spears of English asparagus, medium to large grade
5 slices of white bread, crusts removed
80g (3oz) sliced air-dried ham
50g (¼ cup) unsalted butter, softened
200ml (1 cup) Sauce Gribiche

1 Peel or trim any small leaves from the asparagus and snap off the woody ends.

2 Bring a pan of salted water to the boil. Carefully add the asparagus spears, bring back to the boil and simmer until just tender (3–4 minutes). Remove the asparagus and refresh in ice water and drain on a clean towel.

3 Butter the bread and cut each slice in half, then wrap a slice of bread around the bottom of 10 of the asparagus spears (1 piece per spear). Wrap the remaining asparagus in the ham, making sure that you don't overlap the ham too much as it can be difficult to bite through if it is too thick. Serve with Sauce Gribiche.

Sauce Gribiche

4 freshly cooked hard-boiled free-range egg yolks
1 teaspoon Dijon mustard
250ml (1 cup) groundnut or sunflower oil
1 tablespoon white wine vinegar
2 whites of the hard-boiled eggs, chopped
2 tablespoons small capers, drained and chopped
2 tablespoons cornichons, finely chopped
2 tablespoons soft herbs (chives, tarragon and parsley), chopped
salt and pepper

1 Put the yolks, mustard, salt and pepper in a mortar and crush with the pestle into a smooth paste. Trickle in the oil as you mix, taking care that it amalgamates thoroughly. Add the vinegar in the same way. Then add the remaining ingredients and mix with a spoon. Adjust the seasoning and serve. You can also serve the sauce over plain boiled undressed spears, as illustrated.

Flaked Salmon, Broad Bean and Tarragon Quiche

A deep quiche with a crisp, light pastry case combining the flavours of salmon, broad beans and fresh tarragon. Eat hot or cold with a green salad and boiled new potatoes. Perfect for a light lunch or an afternoon picnic.

Serves 4–6

For the pastry:
125g (1 cup) plain flour
a pinch of salt
25g (⅛ cup) cold butter, diced
25g (⅛ cup) lard
2 tablespoons milk
(Or use 1 × 250g block of ready-made shortcrust pastry)

For the filling:
75ml (⅓ cup) milk
75ml (⅓ cup) double cream
2 medium free-range eggs
1 tablespoon fresh tarragon, chopped
salt and pepper
50g (½ cup) cheddar cheese, grated
100g (¾ cup) poached salmon, flaked
60g (⅓ cup) cooked and shelled broad beans or soya beans

Equipment: 20 cm/8" flan tin

1 Preheat the oven to 190°C (375°F, gas mark 5).

2 To make the pastry, sieve the flour and salt into a bowl, add the fats and rub the mixture through your fingertips until you get a sandy, breadcrumb-like texture. Add the milk a little at a time and bring the ingredients together into a dough. Cover and allow to rest in the fridge for 30–45 minutes.

3 Lightly flour the work surface and roll out the pastry to make a circle a little larger than the top of your flan tin and approximately 0.5 cm thick. Line the tin with the pastry, taking care not to make any holes in it or the filling will leak. Cover and rest for a further 30 minutes in the fridge.

4 Line the pastry case with baking paper, add baking beans and bake blind for 15 minutes. Remove from the oven and take out the baking paper and beans.

5 Reduce the oven temperature to 150°C/300°F/gas mark 2.

6 Beat together the milk, cream, eggs, herbs and seasoning. Scatter half of the grated cheese in the blind-baked pastry case, top with the flaked salmon and beans, and then pour over the milk-and-egg mix. If required, give the filling a gentle stir to ensure it is is evenly dispersed, but again be careful not to damage the pastry case. Sprinkle over the remaining cheese. Place into the oven and bake for 20–25 minutes until set and lightly golden.

Grilled Vegetable Focaccia Loaf

1 500g (1lb 2oz) round focaccia loaf
(approximately 20 cm/8" in diameter)
3 red peppers
3 yellow peppers
4 courgettes
1 aubergine
4 large ripe vine or plum tomatoes
5 tablespoons olive oil
3 teaspoons sherry vinegar
1 garlic clove, smashed
3–4 tablespoons ready-made pesto
½ bunch basil leaves, roughly torn
2 large pinches of sea salt and black pepper

1 Heat the grill or barbeque, depending on how you wish to cook the vegetables (we feel that you get an enhanced flavour from the barbeque). Put the peppers on the grill and allow them to blacken before removing and placing in a plastic bag to continue steaming (this helps to remove the skins).

2 Mix half the olive oil, the crushed garlic and salt and pepper together. Slice the courgettes and aubergine lengthwise into 0.5–0.75 cm slices and mix in with the oil and seasoning. Mix well to ensure the seasoning is evenly dispersed and then discard the garlic. Grill the aubergine and courgette slices until just cooked, and place in a tray.

3 Blanch the tomatoes in boiling water for ten seconds and then refresh in cold water. Remove their skins, which should now slip off easily, and slice them into 1 cm thick slices. Add to the tray with the courgettes and aubergines.

4 Remove the skin from the charred peppers (it should just wash off), discard the seeds, and break the flesh into long strips. Add these to the other vegetables. Mix together the remaining olive oil, sherry vinegar, pesto and torn basil leaves and pour over the vegetables, turning them carefully to make sure they don't get crushed. Adjust the seasoning to taste.

5 Cut the top off the loaf of focaccia, approximately 2 cm from the top. With a small knife, cut around the inside of the loaf leaving approximately 1 cm of bread intact around the crust. Carefully hollow out the loaf, removing the middle, and leaving approximately 1–2 cm intact at the bottom of the loaf. Now start to pack the grilled vegetables carefully into the cavity in the focaccia until the loaf is filled. Put the top back on the loaf and wrap tightly with cling film, ensuring that it is well sealed. Allow to sit overnight before serving cut into wedges.

Hot Cross Buns

Delicious spicy Hot Cross Buns and a slice of rich Simnel Cake are traditional treats for an Easter teatime. Traditionally eaten on Good Friday, Hot Cross Buns are first supposed to have been made by a monk in St Albans Abbey in the 14th century, to distribute to the poor.

1.5 free-range eggs
25g (⅛ cup) fresh yeast
375g (3 cups) strong flour
2 tablespoons unrefined caster sugar
60g (¼ cup) unsalted butter, chilled and diced
a generous pinch of salt
130ml (½ cup) tepid water
2 tablespoons candied mixed peel
2 tablespoons golden sultanas
2 tablespoons raisins
2 teaspoons ground mixed spice

For the piping paste:
4 tablespoons plain white flour
1 tablespoon unrefined caster sugar
1 tablespoon cold water

For the sugar syrup:
100ml (½ cup) water
200g (1 cup) unrefined caster sugar

Equipment: piping bag

1 Preheat the oven to 220ºC (425ºF, gas mark 7).

2 Disperse the yeast in the tepid water. Sieve the flour, salt, sugar and mixed spice into a large mixing bowl, and then rub in the diced butter. Use your fingertips until all the butter has been incorporated into the flour.

3 Make a well in the centre of the mixture. Place the eggs and dispersed yeast into a small bowl and mix together before pouring into the well in the centre of the dry ingredients. Mix together to form a soft pliable dough.

4 Turn the dough out on to a lightly floured work surface and carefully incorporate the dried fruit into the dough. Knead the dough for a further 5 minutes, or until it feels smooth and elastic. Shape the dough into a ball and return it to a clean mixing bowl. Cover the mixing bowl with cling film or a damp clean tea towel, and set aside in a warm area for about 1 hour to prove. The dough should at least double in size.

5 Once the dough has doubled in size it needs knocking back. Set it on a lightly floured surface again and knock the air out of the dough before dividing into 15 evenly sized buns. You can weigh them on a set of scales to ensure consistent sizes; you will need about 50 grams of dough per bun.

recipe continued overleaf

Hot Cross Buns *continued*

6 Roll each piece of dough into a ball and place on to a lined baking tray. Be sure to leave a sufficient space around each bun to allow room as they prove again. Cover with a clean tea towel and allow to prove in a warm area of your kitchen, until they have once more doubled in size. The time this takes will depend upon how warm your kitchen is, but assume around 30–45 minutes.

7 Mix together all of the ingredients for the piping paste to form a paste with a consistency that will allow you to pipe a cross on to each bun. Pipe the crosses, then place the buns on the middle shelf of the preheated oven and bake for 8–12 minutes, or until they turn a pale golden brown. Whilst they bake, boil together the sugar and water to make the sugar syrup. As soon as you remove the buns from the oven, brush them with the warm sugar syrup and set aside to cool on a wire rack.

Opposite: Simnel Cake
(recipe overleaf)

Simnel Cake

3 free-range eggs, whisked together
175g (¾ cup) light muscovado sugar
175g (¾ cup) unsalted butter, softened
1 teaspoon ground mixed spice
175g (1⅓ cups) self-raising flour, sieved
zest of 1 unwaxed lemon
zest of 1 orange
175g (¾ cup) golden sultanas
2 tablespoons candied mixed peel
90g (½ cup) glacé cherries, halved
45g (¼ cup) golden currants
45g (¼ cup) raisins

500g/1lb 2oz almond paste
(you will need to make 11 balls of
about 8g/0.3oz each, a centre disc of
about 190g/6.7oz, and a top layer of
220g/7.8oz)
2 tablespoons apricot jam

Equipment:
18 cm/7" round deep loose-bottomed
metal cake tin
a length of ribbon to decorate

1 Preheat the oven to 150°C (300°F, gas mark 2).

2 Prepare the cake tin by greasing with butter and lining with baking paper. Place the lined tin on to a flat, heavy-duty baking tray and leave to one side until required.

3 Roll out the 190g of almond paste to a circle of 17 cm in diameter (just short of the full width of the cake tin). Cover with cling film and place to one side.

4 Cream together the butter, sugar and citrus zest until light and fluffy. Gradually add the whisked eggs. If the mixture looks like it is splitting, add a little of the sieved flour. Once all the eggs have been added, carefully and evenly fold through the remaining dry ingredients.

5 Spoon half of the cake mixture into the prepared tin and smooth the surface. Carefully place the 17 cm almond paste disc on the top of the cake mix. Spoon the remaining cake mixture on top and level the surface.

6 Place on the middle shelf of the preheated oven and bake for approximately 2 hours, or until golden brown and firm to the touch. Cover the top of the cake with baking paper if it starts to brown too quickly. Once baked, remove from the oven and allow to cool before removing from the tin and taking off the baking paper. Then leave to cool completely.

To decorate the Simnel Cake:

7 Warm the apricot jam and using a pastry brush, brush it over the top of the cake. Roll the 220g almond paste into an 18 cm circular disc – you can use the bottom of the cake tin as a guide to cut around. Place the disc on top of the cake. With the remaining marzipan, prepare 11 × 8g evenly rolled balls (these represent the 11 apostles if serving the cake over the Easter period) and place evenly around the edge of the top of the cake. Once in position they can be gently 'glued' in place with a spot of the remaining apricot jam.

8 To finalise the presentation, the almond paste can be glazed by either placing under a hot grill for one or two minutes until it has browned or by using a blow torch. Adorn with a pretty coloured ribbon and place on to a cake stand – and enjoy.

Individual Lemon Drizzle Cakes

2 free-range eggs
170g (⅞ cup) unrefined caster sugar
170g (¾ cup) unsalted butter, softened
a pinch of salt
170g (1⅓ cups) self-raising flour
zest and juice from 2 unwaxed lemons
90g (⅔ cup) icing sugar, sieved

Equipment:
individual paper loaf moulds, available
from all good supermarkets

1 Preheat the oven to 170°C (325°F, gas mark 3).

2 Place the individual loaf moulds on to a flat, heavy-duty baking tray and leave to one side until required.

3 Place the softened butter in an electric mixer bowl fitted with the whisk attachment. Add the remaining ingredients into the bowl and mix on speed 2 for three minutes until all the ingredients are fully incorporated and aerated. Divide evenly between the loaf moulds.

4 Place on the middle shelf of the preheated oven and bake for about 15 minutes, or until the sponge turns golden brown and springs back when touched.

For the lemon drizzle:

5 Place the lemon juice and the sieved icing sugar into a pan and simmer for a couple of minutes or until translucent in appearance. Brush over the lemon cakes as soon as they come out of the oven so that the liquid soaks evenly throughout the cake.

Yorkshire Rhubarb
Crème Brûlée Tartlets
(recipe overleaf)

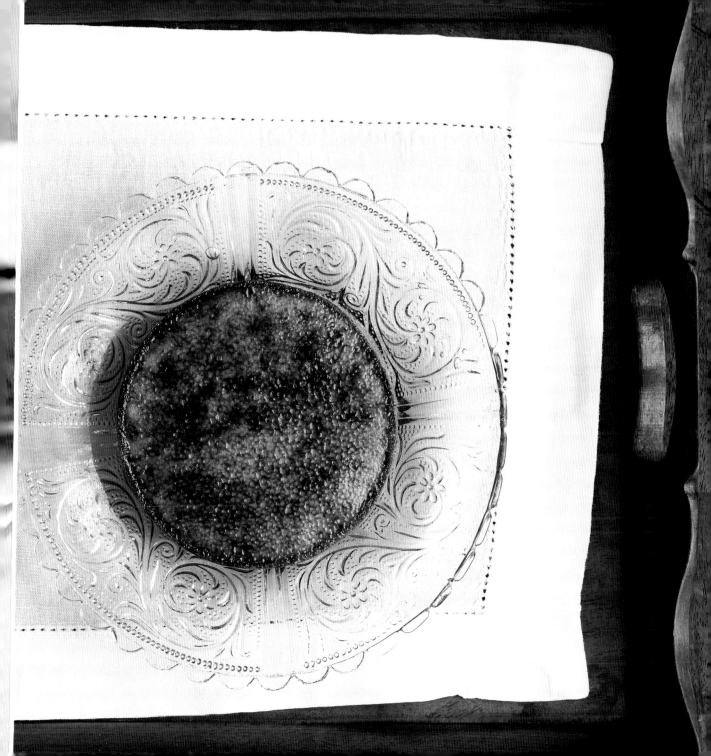

SUMMER

Brioche Crayfish Cocktail Buns

The brioche dough can be used for sweet patisserie, or as here combined with the delicate flavour of crayfish for a luxurious and very special summer treat. This recipe makes at least 20 cocktail-size rolls.

For the brioche dough:
250g (2 cups) strong flour
2 tablespoons unrefined caster sugar
1 teaspoon salt
120g (½ cup) unsalted butter, softened
3 free-range eggs
10g (3 teaspoons) fresh yeast
(or 1½ teaspoons dried yeast)
water to disperse the yeast

For the egg wash:
2 free-range egg yolks
20ml (1 tablespoon) milk

For the filling:
40 crayfish tails
1 gem lettuce (picked, washed, and finely shredded)
4 tablespoons mayonnaise
dash of Tabasco sauce
1 teaspoon Worcestershire sauce
2 dessert spoons tomato ketchup
juice of ½ lemon
½ bunch chives, chopped

Equipment:
electric mixer with dough hook attachment

1 Preheat the oven to 190ºC (375ºF, gas mark 5).

2 Disperse the yeast in a teaspoon of warm water. Sieve the flour, sugar and salt into the electric mixing bowl. Add the dispersed yeast and whole eggs. Using the dough hook, mix until the dough has formed. Next slowly add the softened butter and continue mixing. Cover the dough in the bowl with a damp clean cloth and allow to prove in a warm area of your kitchen.

3 Once proved, knock the dough back, before resting in the fridge for an hour.

4 Once the dough is firm and easier to handle, start to weigh, shape and form the brioche rolls. Use between 10–15 grams of dough for each roll, depending on your appetite and the occasion. Place the rolls onto a greased baking tray, brush over with egg wash, loosely cover with cling film and allow to prove until doubled in size.

5 Once proved, brush with egg wash again, place on the middle shelf of the preheated oven and bake the rolls for 12 minutes, or until golden brown. Remove from the oven and allow to cool on a wire rack.

6 Slice the tops off the brioche rolls and set aside. With a small pointed knife hollow out the main part of the roll (keep for breadcrumbs – see the recipe on page 89). Cover the hollowed-out rolls and set to one side. Mix the mayonnaise with the ketchup, Tabasco and Worcestershire sauces to make a cocktail sauce. Lightly chop the crayfish tails into small chunks.

7 In a bowl mix the chopped crayfish and gem lettuce together, then add the sauce a little at a time, so as to just bind the mixture together. When the mixture is to your liking, add in the chives and then spoon the mixture into the hollowed brioche rolls. Replace the tops on the rolls and serve.

Grilled Sardines with Salsa Verde

Buy the freshest fish you can find for the best results with this dish. Choose sardines with the brightest eyes and the stiffest, shiniest bodies – these are all good signs of freshness.

4–8 sardines depending on the size of the fish (and your appetite), scaled and gutted
100ml (½ cup) extra virgin olive oil
zest and juice of 1 lemon
a pinch of smoked paprika
sea salt and freshly ground black pepper
2 garlic cloves, finely sliced (optional)
¼ bunch fresh lemon thyme
a large sprig of rosemary
salsa verde
1 lemon, cut into wedges to garnish

1 Take the thyme and rosemary and place sprigs of each inside the sardines, then sit the fish in a deep grill pan. Mix together the olive oil, the juice and zest of the lemon, salt, pepper and paprika (and the garlic, if using) and pour over the sardines. Leave the fish in the oil and herb marinade for at least 30 minutes, turning them to ensure they are evenly coated.

2 Under a hot grill cook the sardines for 3–5 minutes on one side before gently turning and cooking for a further 3–5 minutes on the other. Serve immediately with salsa verde and lemon wedges.

Salsa Verde

1 garlic clove, peeled and roughly chopped
1 small bunch flat-leaf parsley, leaves stripped from stalks
1 small bunch basil
1 small bunch mint, leaves stripped from stalks
2 salted anchovies
2 teaspoons capers (salted)
1 teaspoon Dijon mustard
2 dessert spoons red wine vinegar
a few drops of lemon juice
½ teaspoon sugar
a pinch of sea salt
freshly ground black pepper
2 tablespoons olive oil

1 Finely chop the garlic and herbs together. Add the anchovies and capers and continue chopping until everything is well combined. Then add the mustard, lemon juice, red wine vinegar, sugar, salt and pepper into the herb mixture. Stir in the olive oil a little at a time, until you have a sauce with a thick, shiny consistency. You can make this in a food processor, but be careful not to blend the ingredients too finely. The choice of herbs can be adjusted according to your taste and also to make use of what is currently available.

Smoked Sea Trout Parcels

This delicious dish makes a delicate starter for two, or it can be served with a light salad, some sliced avocado and perhaps some granary or soda bread.

250g (9oz) sliced smoked sea trout or smoked salmon
zest and juice of ½ lemon
150ml (⅝ cup) double cream
a pinch of cayenne pepper
1 teaspoon horseradish cream
100ml (½ cup) crème fraîche
1 teaspoon chives, chopped
4 small sprigs of dill

1 Cut the sliced smoked sea trout into 4 rectangles of 10 × 8 cm, laying each slice on baking paper. Dice all of the remaining trout, add the lemon juice and blend in the food processor until it forms a very fine paste (taking care not to overheat the mixture in the processor). Chill the mixture, still in the processor bowl, for 20 minutes. Scrape the sides of the bowl and, returning the bowl to the processor, gently add the cream into the paste on pulse, taking time to stir between additions. Ensure that the mixture is not worked too much or it will split and become grainy in texture. Gently fold in the lemon zest and set aside.

2 Take your slices of smoked sea trout and place a large tablespoon of the mousse in the centre and then gently fold over the edges to create neat, evenly shaped parcels. Allow the parcels to set in the fridge for 20–30 minutes.

3 Add the chopped chives and horseradish to the crème fraîche, mixing to make a sauce to serve alongside the parcels.

4 Garnish the parcels with a sprig of dill and a dollop of the crème fraîche sauce.

Egg Mayonnaise on Toast Points

Incredibly simple but when made with beautiful fresh eggs and unctuous home-made mayonnaise, this dish is a real treat on a summer's afternoon.

4 fresh free-range eggs
3 tablespoons home-made mayonnaise
1 teaspoon English mustard (optional)
1 small bunch fresh watercress (washed and picked through)
4 slices of thinly sliced granary bread
salt and pepper

1 Depending on how thin you want your toast 'points' to be, you may want to grill the bread, remove the crusts, and then separate the toasted sides of the bread from each other with the round end of a knife, in the same way as for Melba toast. Then cut each side into quarters and put on to a tray, untoasted side up, and grill again.

2 Boil the eggs for 6 minutes, remove from the water and allow to cool slightly. Peel the shell from the eggs over a bowl, and halve and chop the eggs, not too finely, into a bowl. Gently fold in the mayonnaise (and the extra mustard if using), adjust the seasoning, and fold in half of the watercress.

3 Spoon the egg mayonnaise on to the toast points, garnish with the remaining watercress.

Home-made Mayonnaise

3 free-range egg yolks (as fresh as possible)
1 tablespoon Dijon mustard
1 teaspoon salt
freshly ground white pepper
2 tablespoons tarragon vinegar
450ml (2 cups) groundnut oil

1 Place a bowl on a tea towel to hold it steady, and in it whisk together the egg yolks, mustard, half the tarragon vinegar, salt and a little freshly ground pepper. When thoroughly combined and starting to go a paler colour, start to add the oil in a steady stream a little at a time (best poured from a measuring jug, even better if someone else can help you). This is the critical point – too much oil too quickly and the mixture will curdle.

2 As the mixture starts to thicken, add the remainder of the tarragon vinegar to loosen the mixture again slightly, then add the remainder of the oil in a slow steady stream. Adjust the seasoning to taste. You can store home-made mayonnaise in the fridge for up to 5 days.

Overleaf: Scones and strawberry jam

Victoria Sponge

Another wonderful way to show off home-made jam. Queen Victoria is known to have had a sweet tooth, and this light but delicious cake was named in her honour.

For the Victoria sponge:
3 free-range eggs
150g (¾ cup) unrefined caster sugar
150g (⅔ cup) unsalted butter, softened
150g (1¼ cups) self-raising flour, sieved
½ teaspoon of vanilla essence

For the vanilla buttercream:
150g (⅔ cup) unsalted butter, softened
220g (1¾ cups) icing sugar, sieved
⅓ split vanilla pod

home-made strawberry jam
(see page 53)

Equipment:
2 × 20 cm/8" Victoria sponge cake tins

1 Preheat the oven to 180°C (350°F, gas mark 4).

2 Prepare the cake tins by greasing with butter and lining the bottom with a circular piece of baking paper. Leave to one side until required.

3 Cream together the caster sugar, vanilla essence and softened butter in a bowl until light and fluffy. Gradually add the beaten eggs, a little at a time to avoid the mixture curdling. Finally, fold through the sieved flour until all the ingredients are perfectly combined.

4 Divide the cake mix evenly between the two prepared cake tins and carefully smooth the mix to create two level layers. Place on the middle shelf of the preheated oven and bake for approximately 20 minutes or until the cake appears golden brown and an inserted skewer comes out clean. Once baked, remove from the oven and allow to cool slightly before turning the cakes out on to a wire rack.

To make the buttercream:

5 Cream the softened butter with the sieved icing sugar and the seeds from the split vanilla pod. The buttercream will become pale and fluffy with little flecks of vanilla seeds throughout.

To assemble the Victoria sponge:

6 Once the cakes have completely cooled, carefully and evenly spread a layer of buttercream on to the top of the first cake. Next add a thick layer of your home-made jam, before carefully placing the second cake on top of the jam and very gently pressing down. Finally, dust the top of the cake with icing sugar.

7 Serve with a pot of tea!

Cherry Madeleines

The French writer Marcel Proust made these dainty little cakes famous. There is something delightfully chic about a plate of madeleines; these, with half a fresh cherry apiece, are particularly special. Madeleines are best eaten slightly warm, and definitely on the day of baking.

90g (½ cup) unrefined caster sugar
3 free-range egg whites
90g (⅜ cup) unsalted butter
35g (¼ cup) ground almonds
35g (¼ cup) plain flour
5 fresh cherries

Equipment:
non-stick silicone madeleine mould

1 Preheat the oven to 190°C (375°F, gas mark 5).

2 Prepare the madeleine mould by greasing with softened butter and dusting with flour. Place the lined tin on to a flat, heavy-duty baking tray and leave to one side until required.

3 Place the unsalted butter into a saucepan and gently heat until it turns a nut-brown colour, exuding a rich nutty smell. Immediately remove the 'beurre noisette' (as it is now known) from the saucepan to stop the cooking process, and allow to cool slightly.

4 In a separate bowl whisk together the egg whites, caster sugar, plain flour and ground almonds until light and fluffy. Carefully and slowly add the beurre noisette and continue to whisk until smooth. Place the madeleine mix in the fridge and chill for 30 minutes.

5 Wash and stone the fresh cherries and cut them into halves. Remove the madeleine mix from the fridge and give it a stir. Fill the prepared madeleine moulds almost to the top then carefully place half a cherry into each mould. Try not to push the cherry down as it will then sink during baking.

6 Place on the middle shelf of the preheated oven and bake for approximately 12 minutes, or until the madeleine turns a light golden brown. Once baked remove from the oven and allow to cool before removing from the madeleine mould and placing on a wire rack.

Summer Berry Tartlets

This uses the same sweet pastry recipe as the Yorkshire Rhubarb Crème Brûlée Tartlets, on page 36. Filling the tartlets with wild strawberries as suggested here adds a truly decadent feel to any afternoon tea, but any summer berries will work perfectly well.

350g (12oz) sweet pastry (see page 36).

For the crème pâtissière:
170ml (¾ cup) milk
1.5 free-range egg yolks
40g (¼ cup) unrefined caster sugar
8g (1 dessert spoon) unsalted butter, chilled and cut into cubes
9g (1 dessert spoon) cornflour
1 split vanilla pod

100g (3½oz) white chocolate, melted
assorted summer berries:
wild strawberries, redcurrants, raspberries, blueberries

Equipment:
individual 5 cm/2" tartlet moulds, piping bag, 6 cm/2.5" plain cutter

1 Preheat the oven to 190ºC (375ºF, gas mark 5).

2 Roll the sweet pastry out on a lightly floured surface to a thickness of 2 mm. Place on a tray and rest in the fridge for 20–30 minutes. (Resting the pastry between each step will reduce the risk of the pastry shrinking during baking.)

3 Cut out the pastry discs for the tartlets and line the moulds carefully. Allow to rest in the fridge for another 20–30 minutes before trimming the edges.

4 Blind-bake the tartlets using ceramic beads in the middle of the oven for approximately 15 minutes, until they start to go golden around the edges. Carefully remove the ceramic beads and continue baking until the tartlets are an even golden colour. Remove from the oven and allow them to cool on a wire rack.

5 For the crème pâtissière, bring the milk to the boil with the split vanilla pod and remove from the heat.

6 Whisk together the egg yolks and sugar until they are pale and fluffy. Fold in the cornflour before adding the hot milk, stirring all the while. Pour the mixture back into the pan and return to the heat, stirring it until it starts to thicken. Cook for another 3 minutes before gently stirring in the diced butter. Set aside to cool, covering with cling film to prevent a skin from forming, then chill in the fridge till required.

7 Carefully brush the inside of the tartlets with the melted white chocolate. Allow the chocolate time to set before the next step.

8 Fill each tartlet ⅔ of the way up with the crème pâtissière before topping with your choice of summer berries.

AUTUMN

Game Pâté

Long walks on an autumn afternoon deserve something properly substantial for tea. This pâté can be made from any leftover cooked game. Adjust the quantities of the other ingredients relative to the size of the bird you use.

1 game bird of your choice (partridge, grouse or pheasant)
1 teaspoon redcurrant jelly
50ml (¼ cup) game sauce or chicken stock
1 dash sherry
175–250ml (¾–1 cup) double cream
100g (½ cup) unsalted butter
salt and pepper to taste

1 Take all the meat off the carcass, taking care to remove any lead shot. Remove and discard the skin, then dice the meat. Place the diced meat in a food processor along with the sherry, the redcurrant jelly, and game sauce, and then blend the game meat to a fine purée. Chill in the processor before stirring in the double cream, a little at a time, until you reach a spreadable consistency. Adjust the seasoning to taste before putting the pâté into the serving dish and chilling.

2 Melt the butter and pour over the top of the cold pâté in a thin layer and chill again. Serve with thin Melba toast (see page 49).

Miniature Game Pies

500g (1lb 2oz) assorted game (partridge, venison, pheasant), diced into 2 cm chunks and seasoned

2 carrots, peeled and diced into ½ cm pieces

2 sticks celery, peeled and diced into ½ cm pieces

1 onion, peeled and finely chopped

150g (5oz) button mushrooms, quartered

100g (3½oz) smoked bacon, cut into 0.5 cm lardons

2 bay leaves

½ bunch thyme

250g (2 cups) plain flour

1 teaspoon tomato purée

100ml (⅜ cup) red wine

570ml (2⅜ cups) chicken or game stock

salt and pepper

cooking oil

500g (1lb 2oz) ready prepared puff pastry

Equipment:
fluted cutters, 12-hole bun tray

1 In a heavy-bottomed pan heat the oil, and when hot add the diced game and the bacon lardons and colour gently. Remove the meat and set aside. Next add the vegetables and herbs to the pan and sweat down gently, without colouring, until softened. Add the tomato purée and flour and cook for 2–3 minutes, stirring all the time. Then add the red wine and continue to cook until the liquid has reduced by two thirds. Return the meat to the pan, add the stock and bring to a boil. Skim off the surface of the mixture, reduce the heat so it cools to a simmer and then cook for approximately 30 minutes. Adjust the seasoning and consistency of the sauce – it should be thick enough to coat the back of a spoon.

2 Roll out the puff pastry to 3 mm thick, and cut out discs of 6–7 cm in diameter using a fluted cutter. Line the bun tray with discs and then add a good spoonful of the game mix to each one. Egg-wash the edges and put on the top disc of the pastry. Crimp together and rest in the fridge for 30 minutes. At this point, preheat the oven to 180°C (350°F, gas mark 4). Remove the tray from the fridge, brush the pies with egg wash and bake for 20 minutes.

Miniature Sausage Rolls

Makes 10 rolls

260g (9oz) sausagemeat
180g (6oz) ready prepared all-butter puff pastry
1 fresh egg
1 bunch sage, chopped
1 small onion, finely chopped
2 teaspoons vegetable oil
2–3 tablespoons flour, for dusting

1 Sweat the chopped onion in the oil for 5 minutes without letting it colour, then add the chopped sage and cook for a further 2 minutes. Remove the onion and sage from the heat and allow to cool before mixing into the sausagemeat. Place the sausagemeat in a piping bag with a small nozzle.

2 On a floured surface roll out the pastry until it is about 3 mm thick. Move the pastry sheet to a clean surface. Pipe sausagemeat along one edge of the pastry, leaving a 1 cm gap before the edge itself. Fold the pastry over the sausagemeat and seal the edges together with egg wash. Trim the pastry to neaten the edge, then allow to firm in the fridge for 45 minutes.

3 Preheat the oven to 200°C (400°F, gas mark 6).

4 Cut the long sausage roll into 4 cm slices. Place on a baking tray and bake for 10 minutes until golden brown.

Opposite: Wild Mushroom Vol-au-vents

Wild Mushroom Vol-au-vents

Scottish girolles are delicious in this recipe when in season, but otherwise you can use any variety of wild mushrooms.

500g (1lb 2oz) assorted wild mushrooms (Scottish girolles when in season), cleaned
1 clove garlic, crushed
150g (5oz) shallots, chopped
½ bunch tarragon, chopped
175ml (¾ cup) double cream
70ml (¼ cup) olive oil
salt and pepper
12 vol-au-vent cases

Chop the mushrooms into 0.5 cm pieces. Heat the oil until it is hot, but not smoking, and then add the mushrooms along with the shallots and garlic and sauté. Add the cream and reduce until the consistency is just thick enough to coat a spoon, then adjust the seasoning, remove from the heat and add the tarragon. Fill the vol-au-vent cases with the mushroom mixture and serve immediately.

Smoked Haddock Kedgeree

There are many ways to prepare kedgeree. Some like a more piquant version, with curry spices, while others enjoy a simpler version, highlighting the natural flavour of the smoked haddock.

Serves 10

1.2kg (2lb 10oz) smoked haddock fillets (natural undyed)
5 free-range eggs
500g (2¼ cups) long-grain rice
1 large onion, peeled
2 cloves garlic
2 bay leaves
500ml (2 cups) milk
350ml (1½ cups) double cream
100g (½ cup) unsalted butter
2 teaspoons mild curry powder (optional)
1 teaspoon ground cumin (optional)
350g (12oz) fresh chanterelle or button mushrooms, cleaned
1 bunch parsley or coriander (depending on your preference), chopped

1 Mix the milk and cream and infuse with half the onion, half the garlic and the bay leaves on the stove, bringing it up to a gentle simmer. Skin and remove any pin bones from the smoked haddock fillets, before cutting into 10 good portions of 90 grams each, retaining all the trimmings.

2 Cook the rice until just tender in boiling salted water, rinse and reserve. Soft-boil the eggs (5 minutes), peel and keep warm until required.

3 Finely chop the remaining onion and garlic, then gently sweat in the butter, taking care not to colour. If using the spices add these to the onions now and cook out gently for a further 2–3 minutes before adding the mushrooms. Whilst the onion and spices are sweating, gently add all the fish (portions and trimmings) to the milk and cream mixture and cook until just firm to the touch. Remove the portions and set aside on a separate plate.

4 Add the cooked rice to the onion and spice mixture and fold in well, ensuring that the rice is evenly coated with the spices. Next add enough of the milk and cream mixture (including the trimmings of haddock) to bind the rice. You are aiming for a creamy risotto-like dish. Check and adjust the seasoning to your liking and, finally, add the chopped herbs.

5 Carefully spoon the kedgeree mixture into the serving dish before arranging the quartered eggs and haddock portions on top.

Baked Autumnal Fruit Tart

The fruit in this tart can be quince, plums, pears, apples or blackberries. Firm fruit needs to be gently poached before using. Again, the sweet pastry recipe on page 36 will give an excellent result here.

2 free-range eggs at room temperature
125g (⅔ cup) unrefined caster sugar
125g (½ cup) butter, softened
110g (⅞ cup) ground almonds
zest of 1 unwaxed lemon
15g (1 tablespoon) plain flour
75g (¼ cup) plum preserve
fruit in season, gently poached

Equipment:
20 cm/8" metal tart ring

1 Preheat the oven to 170°C (325°F, gas mark 3).

2 Prepare the metal tart ring by greasing with butter and lining with sweet pastry. Place the lined ring on to a flat, heavy-duty baking tray lined with baking paper and leave in the fridge until required.

3 Place the softened butter, sugar and lemon zest in a mixing bowl and beat until light and fluffy. Gradually add the eggs and then finally fold through the flour and ground almonds.

4 Take the pastry shell out of the fridge and prick the bottom with a fork. Evenly spread the plum jam on to the base before filling with the almond cream mix. Smooth the almond cream and then arrange the poached fruit of choice attractively on the top.

5 Place on the middle shelf of the preheated oven and bake for approximately 35 minutes, or until golden brown. Once baked, remove from the oven and allow to cool before removing the ring and the baking paper.

Carrot Cake

This is a dark, spicy cake, deliciously moist and very moreish.

2 small free-range eggs
105g (½ cup) dark brown sugar
105g (½ cup) soft brown sugar
150g (1⅛ cups) wholemeal flour
¼ teaspoon salt
½ teaspoon bicarbonate of soda
½ teaspoon ground nutmeg
1 teaspoon ground cinnamon
35g (⅛ cup) sour cream
105g (⅜ cup) sunflower oil
180g (3 cups) carrots, grated
45g (½ cup) desiccated coconut

For the cream cheese topping:
110g (½ cup) full-fat soft cream cheese
50g (¼ cup) unsalted butter
50g (⅓ cup) icing sugar
juice of ½ lemon

Equipment:
18 cm/7" cake tin

1 Preheat the oven to 170°C (325°F, gas mark 3).

2 Prepare the cake tin by greasing with butter and lining the bottom and sides with baking paper. Place the lined tin on to a flat, heavy-duty baking tray and leave to one side until required.

3 Whisk together the eggs, sugars and sunflower oil in a bowl until thoroughly mixed. In a separate bowl, sift together the flour, salt, bicarbonate of soda and spices. Fold the dry ingredients into the egg mix until all ingredients are combined evenly. Finally, fold through the grated carrots and sour cream.

4 Pour the carrot cake mix into the lined cake tin. Place on the middle shelf of the preheated oven and bake for approximately 35 minutes, or until the cake springs back when touched. Once baked remove from the oven and allow to cool on a wire rack.

For the cream cheese topping:

5 Sift the icing sugar into a bowl and add the softened butter. Beat well until light and fluffy. Add the cream cheese and continue beating until a smooth consistency is achieved. Finally, slowly add the lemon juice whilst still mixing.

To assemble the carrot cake:

6 Once completely cool, remove the carrot cake from the cake tin and place on your desired serving plate or cake stand. Using a palette knife, carefully smooth the cream cheese topping evenly across the top of the cake.

Cardamom and Orange Shortbread

Cardamom adds an unusual citrus flavour to this delicate shortbread, and so combines beautifully with the orange zest.

135g (2/3 cup) unrefined caster sugar
240g (1 cup) unsalted butter, softened
330g (2½ cups) plain flour, sieved
30g (3 tablespoons) rice flour, sieved
zest of 1 unwaxed orange
10g (1 tablespoon) ground cardamom

Equipment:
shortbread mould (see illustration on the Contents page), or plain biscuit cutters

1 Preheat the oven to 180°C (350°F, gas mark 4).

2 Place the softened butter and sugar into a bowl and beat until light and fluffy. Add the orange zest and ground cardamom before carefully folding through the sieved flours. Allow to rest in the refrigerator before rolling on to a lightly floured surface to 0.5 cm thick. Cut out, and gently place on a tray lined with baking paper.

3 Place on the middle shelf of the preheated oven and bake for approximately 8 minutes. The shortbread will turn a light sandy colour when baked – do not allow the shortbread to become any darker than that. Remove from the oven and carefully place the shortbread on a wire rack to cool, sprinkling with caster sugar immediately.

Tea Bread

Tea bread can be enjoyed just as it is, but is equally moreish with jam, or even with cheese.

150ml (⅝ cup) boiling water
2 Earl Grey teabags
120g (⅝ cup) soft brown sugar
250g (1¼ cups) mixed dried fruit
(golden sultanas, dried apricots, raisins and currants)
180g (1⅓ cups) plain flour
1 teaspoon baking powder
1 teaspoon ground mixed spice
1.5 free-range eggs (75g)
warmed honey to glaze

Equipment:
900g/2lb loaf tin

1 Pour the boiling water over the teabags and allow to infuse for 10 minutes, then remove the teabags, add the sugar and the dried fruit. Ideally leave the fruit to soak for 12 hours.

2 Preheat the oven to 170°C (325°F, gas mark 3).

3 Prepare the metal loaf tin by greasing with butter and lining the bottom and sides with baking paper. Place the lined tin on to a flat, heavy-duty baking tray and leave to one side until required.

4 Mix all of the dry ingredients in a bowl, then add the eggs and soaked fruit. Once all the ingredients are fully combined, spoon into the prepared loaf tin. Place on the middle shelf of the preheated oven and bake for 30 minutes, or until the loaf turns a golden brown colour. When the loaf is almost baked, remove from the oven and liberally brush warm honey all over. Return to the oven for a further 10 minutes until a golden glossy appearance is achieved. Allow to cool before removing from the loaf tin.

Quince Cheese

Fruit 'cheese' is the traditional name for preserves made with fruit purée and sugar.

1.5kg (3lb 5oz) quince
1kg (5 cups) granulated sugar
juice of 1 lemon
vegetable oil for brushing jars

1 Wash and clean the quince thoroughly, ensuring that any downy coat is removed from the skins. Chop into evenly sized chunks, leaving in the core (there is plenty of pectin within the pips so the core is good for the jelly). Put the fruit into a wide stainless steel pan and just cover with water (about 1.5 litres). Bring to the boil and then simmer for 2.5–3 hours, until the fruit is soft and has turned a dark rosy colour. You may need to add more water to ensure the fruit is entirely cooked through, but add only a little at a time to avoid having too much liquid in the pan.

2 Once the fruit is very soft, push the mixture through a fine sieve with a ladle to remove any pips and debris (a laborious task but worth it in the end). Measure out the purée and for every 500 grams of quince purée add 500 grams of sugar. Mix together in a wide stainless steel saucepan and heat on a low gentle heat, stirring until the sugar has dissolved before turning up the heat slightly. Keep stirring as the mixture heats and thickens (do take care as it will be very hot and can spit) until it reaches a stage where your spoon can leave a clear line across the bottom of the pan (approximately 30 minutes).

3 Lightly oil the sterilised jars and fill them with the hot quince cheese. Allow to cool before sealing and then keep refrigerated. This is excellent served with cheese or cured meats. You may even like it spread on a hot toasted crumpet – in which case, see page 86.

WINTER

G. IV. REX
1828

Crumpets

Crumpets are one of those foods that belong in a unique category. They evoke special memories for so many people, whether of simply toasting a crumpet in front of a fire on a wet afternoon in your childhood, or just the thought of all that butter trapped in their bubbly texture. They really are worth the extra time and effort it takes to make your own.

175g (1⅓ cups) strong white flour
175g (1⅓ cups) plain flour
2 × 7g sachets instant yeast
1 teaspoon caster sugar
350ml (1½ cups) milk, warmed
150–200ml (⅝–¾ cup) warm water
½ teaspoon bicarbonate of soda
1 teaspoon salt
sunflower oil for cooking

Equipment:
4 metal crumpet rings

1 Weigh the flours into a bowl. Add the yeast and stir through the flour. Dissolve the sugar in the warm milk and pour on to the flour. Using a wooden spoon, beat until you have a smooth batter – this will take 3–4 minutes and is hard work, but is essential to produce the characteristic holes in the cooked crumpets. Cover and leave for at least 20 minutes and up to an hour. The batter will rise and then begin to fall. You will see marks on the side of the bowl to show where the batter was before it dropped.

2 Mix the bicarbonate of soda and salt with the warm water and beat it into the batter. Add about three quarters of the water, and then continue to add a little at a time until you get a mixture with the consistency of double cream. Cover and rest for 20 minutes.

3 Heat a flat griddle or heavy-based pan. Lightly grease the inside of four metal crumpet rings and the griddle. Sit the rings on the griddle over a medium heat. Drop two dessert spoonfuls of mixture into each ring. After 4–5 minutes bubbles should appear and the surface should be set. Carefully turn the crumpets over, still in their rings, and cook for a further 3 minutes.

4 Serve immediately, or leave to cool and then toast before eating with plenty of butter.

Quail Scotch Eggs

When flouring, dipping and breadcrumbing the scotch eggs, the trick is not to do too many at one time – and an extra helping hand is always useful.

12 quail's eggs, uncooked
200g (7oz) of the best-quality black pudding you can source
150g (5oz) minced pork
1 tablespoon fresh herbs (parsley or chives), chopped
1 teaspoon English mustard powder
30g (½ cup) fresh white breadcrumbs
salt and pepper

For the coating:
75g (⅔ cup) plain flour, seasoned with salt and pepper
1 free-range egg
a splash of milk
100g (1⅔ cups) fresh white breadcrumbs
300–450ml (1½ cups) vegetable oil (depending on the size of your pan)

1 Add the quail's eggs to a pan of boiling water and boil for 1½–2 minutes, depending how hard you like your eggs. Refresh in cold water, peel and reserve.

2 Mix the black pudding, pork, herbs, mustard powder and breadcrumbs together in a bowl. Divide into 12 even balls. Take one ball and roll out to a thin layer, add a quail's egg and draw up the mixture to completely cover the egg. Repeat this for each egg and, once completed, chill for 30 minutes.

3 Put the flour in one bowl. Mix the egg and milk together in a second bowl, and put the fresh breadcrumbs in a third. Once the scotch eggs have firmed up in the fridge, coat each egg with flour, dip into the egg mix and then roll carefully in the breadcrumbs.

4 Heat the vegetable oil in a heavy based pan to about 165°C/330°F and carefully drop the breaded scotch eggs into the oil, 3–4 at a time. Once they are lightly golden brown, lift from the oil and drain on absorbent paper. You can add a little more seasoning at this stage, and then serve. The eggs are good eaten with mustard, mayonnaise or ketchup.

Overleaf: Traditional ham

Clementine Macarons

The macaron is an historic teatime treat, which can be traced back to medieval Venice. The fashion of sandwiching two together with a flavoured filling originated in Paris in the early years of the twentieth century.

For the clementine cream:
2 clementines, juice and zest
70g (⅓ cup) refined caster sugar
70g (⅓ cup) unsalted butter, chilled and diced
3 free-range eggs
1 free-range egg yolk

For the macaron shells:
75g/2 free-range egg whites
200g (1½ cups) icing sugar
200g (1¾ cups) ground almonds

200g (1 cup) refined caster sugar
75g/2 free-range egg whites
tangerine food colouring paste

Equipment:
piping bag and 1 cm plain nozzle,
electric thermometer,
3 cm plain cutter, a pencil

To make the clementine cream:

1 Put the clementine zest, juice, sugar, eggs and egg yolk into a heatproof bowl. Sit the bowl over a saucepan of gently simmering water, ensuring that the water is not touching the bottom of the bowl. Continuously stir the mixture until it begins to gently simmer.

2 Remove the bowl of clementine cream from the saucepan and slowly add the cubes of chilled butter, stirring until they have all melted. Pass the mixture through a fine sieve. Set aside to cool, covering directly with cling film to avoid a skin forming. Once chilled, keep in the fridge until required.

To make the macaron shells:

3 Take a sheet of baking paper and cut it to the size of your baking tray. Using a pencil draw around a 3 cm plain cutter, leaving enough room between each round for the macarons to spread. Now place the paper upside down on to the baking tray as your stencil. Leave to one side.

4 Place the first 75g of egg whites, the sieved icing sugar and the ground almonds into a bowl and beat until a paste has formed.

recipe continued overleaf

Gâteau
Opéra *continued*

Equipment:
electric mixer,
2 × Swiss roll baking trays
(39 × 24 cm/15 × 10"),
gold leaf, palette knife, electric
thermometer or sugar thermometer,
25 × 8cm/10 × 3" rectangular mould
or frame (optional), ruler

To make the coffee soaking syrup:

6 Mix the freshly made coffee with the water and sugar, and allow to cool.

To assemble the Gâteau Opéra:

7 Cut the joconde sheets into 6 strips measuring the same dimensions as your rectangular mould (or if assembling freehand just cut the sponge into 6 evenly sized rectangles).

8 Line a flat tray with baking paper and sit the mould on top. Place the first joconde sheet into the rectangular mould and soak generously and evenly with the coffee soaking syrup.

9 Next spread a thin, even layer of chocolate ganache on to the soaked layer of sponge, followed by the next layer of joconde. Ensure that the sponge is pressed down on top of the ganache evenly and securely. Soak the next sponge with the syrup. Repeat the ganache step but using instead the coffee buttercream, spreading a layer the exact thickness of the previous layer of ganache. Repeat this entire process until you get to the last layer of joconde, alternating ganache with coffee buttercream. The last layer will be soaked with the coffee syrup only. See the illustration for the finished effect you are aiming for!

10 Place in the fridge and allow to firm for at least an hour.

11 Once firm, remove the rectangular ring, using a hot dry knife to release the Gâteau Opéra from the edges of the mould. Place the cake on to a clean chopping board. Soften some of the remaining ganache in a microwave until it is a thick pouring consistency. Using a palette knife, spread the warmed ganache on the top of the opéra as thinly and evenly as you can. Return the gâteau to the fridge for the ganache to firm.

To portion and present:

12 Trim the edges of the gâteau with a hot dry knife to ensure the edges are straight before using a ruler to mark out the portion size. Slice the cake into the marked portions again using a hot dry knife. The gâteau illustrated has been cut in to portions of 2.5 × 6 cm (1 × 2.5"), but you can be as generous as you like! Finally, place on your serving dish and decorate with gold leaf.

Winter Biscuits: Brandy Snaps

100g (⅞ cup) icing sugar, sieved
100g (7 tablespoons) unsalted butter, softened
100g (4 tablespoons) liquid glucose
100g (⅞ cup) plain flour, sieved
vegetable oil for greasing

1 Preheat the oven to 200ºC (400ºF, gas mark 6).

2 In a bowl place the softened butter, icing sugar, flour and glucose, and beat vigorously until all of the ingredients come together to form a smooth sticky paste. Place in the fridge in a plastic container until firm enough to handle.

3 Once firm, divide the paste into 10g balls and press down on to a baking tray lined with baking paper. Leave plenty of room around each ball of paste as the mixture will spread considerably. (You will probably need to cook the snaps in several batches.) Place on the middle shelf of the preheated oven and bake for 8 minutes, or until the brandy snap turns golden brown. Whilst they are baking, lightly grease the handle of a wooden spoon with vegetable oil.

4 Remove the tray from the oven and whilst warm but not hot, pick a brandy snap up with a palette knife and carefully roll around the handle of the wooden spoon. Allow to cool slightly before removing from the handle with a careful sliding motion; your biscuit should have taken on the shape of a cigar. Repeat with the rest of the biscuits.

5 Once completely cool store in an airtight container or tin until teatime!

Sablés aux Confiture

You may know these crisp, sweet biscuits as 'Jammy Dodgers'.

1 free-range egg yolk
100g (½ cup) unrefined caster sugar
200g (⅞ cup) softened unsalted butter
250g (2 cups) plain flour
150g (½ cup) seedless raspberry jam
icing sugar for dusting

Equipment:
3 cm/1.25" and 5 cm/2" plain cutters,
small dusting sieve, piping bag

1 Preheat the oven to 160°C (300°F, gas mark 2).

2 Place the softened butter and sugar into a bowl and beat with a spoon until light and fluffy. Slowly mix in the egg yolk before folding through the flour. Wrap the biscuit paste in cling film and rest in the fridge until firm.

3 Once the paste is sufficiently firm, place on to a floured surface and roll out to a thickness of 3–4 mm. Return to the fridge on a tray lined with baking paper and allow to firm for another 30 minutes before cutting. (This is a sticky paste and will require patience and a cool area to work in.)

4 For each biscuit you will require a top and a bottom. Using the 5 cm cutter, cut as many biscuits as possible from your paste and carefully place on a baking tray lined with baking paper. The biscuits shouldn't spread so you can place them quite close together. Return to the fridge before carefully cutting out the centres of half the biscuits with the 3 cm cutter. These will form the tops of your biscuits – make sure the holes are nicely centred.

5 Place the tray on the middle shelf of the preheated oven and bake for approximately 12 minutes, or until the biscuits turn a light sandy colour. Once baked, remove from the oven and allow to cool on a wire cooling rack.

To assemble the sablés aux confiture:

6 Spoon the raspberry jam into the piping bag and snip off the tip of the bag just enough to allow the jam to flow freely. Pipe a circle of jam on to each biscuit base, leaving an edge of about 0.5 cm. Next flood the centre of the jam circle with the jam. Then take the tops of your biscuits, dust them with icing sugar and carefully place each one on to a jam-covered base.

Chocolate and Almond Biscotti

Biscotti are firm dry biscuits, perfect for dipping into a hot drink.
The word biscotti means 'twice baked' in Italian.

3 free-range egg yolks
3 free-range eggs
370g (1⅞ cups) unrefined caster sugar
40g (3 tablespoons) unsalted butter, softened
520g (4 cups) plain flour
2 teaspoons baking powder
zest of 1 unwaxed orange
160g (6oz) whole peeled almonds
160g (6oz) dark chocolate chips

1 Preheat the oven to 170ºC (325ºF, gas mark 3).

2 Place the softened butter, orange zest and sugar into a bowl and beat with a spoon until light and fluffy. Slowly mix in the egg yolks and whole eggs before folding through the seived flour and baking powder. Finally, fold through the almonds and chocolate chips. Wrap the biscuit paste in cling film and place in the fridge to rest.

3 Once firm, roll the paste by hand into cylinders about 3 cm wide and the length of your baking tray. Place on a lined baking tray, leaving enough room between each roll to allow for them to spread in the oven.

4 Sit the tray on the middle shelf of the preheated oven and bake for approximately 12 minutes, or until the biscotti turn a light golden brown. Once baked, remove from the oven and allow to cool slightly before cutting the biscotti diagonally into slices about 1 cm wide. Then return the tray to the oven to bake for a further 5 minutes until firm to the touch.

Overleaf: A Christmas tea, complete with cake and mince pies.

Festive Mince Pies

For the mincemeat:
zest and juice of 1 unwaxed lemon
zest and juice of 1 unwaxed orange
2 tablespoons brandy
1 tablespoon port
1 tablespoon rum
1 tablespoon sherry
120g (1 cup) suet
160g (¾ cup) golden sultanas
100g (½ cup) raisins
100g (½ cup) mixed peel
100g (½ cup) currants
½ teaspoon ground nutmeg
½ teaspoon ground cinnamon
½ teaspoon ground cloves
160g (6oz) russet apples, peeled and grated

500g (1lb 2oz) sweet pastry (see recipe on page 36)

egg wash for sticking lids to bases
granulated sugar for the top of the mince pies before baking
icing sugar for dusting

Equipment:
12 hole non-stick shallow baking tray / mince pie tin 32 × 24 cm/12.5 × 9.5",
fluted or plain cutters (additional shaped cutters are optional)

1 Place all the dry ingredients into a large mixing bowl and stir. Then add all the liquids and grated apple and allow to soak for at least one week in a 1kg kilner jar sat in the fridge or pantry.

2 Preheat the oven to 190ºC (375ºF, gas mark 5).

3 Roll the sweet pastry into a sheet approximately 2 to 3 mm thick, place on a tray, and allow to rest in the fridge. Once rested, cut tops and bottoms for your mince pies using fluted or plain cutters (selecting sizes to fit your tin). Place the pie bases into the tin and prick them with a small knife or fork to prevent the pastry from rising during baking.

4 Spoon a teaspoon of the home-made mincemeat into the base and egg wash the edge of the pastry to enable the lids to stick. Place the mince pies in the fridge to rest for another 30 minutes, then add a pastry top to each, egg washing it and pricking a small hole in the top to allow the steam to escape. Sprinkle with granulated sugar.

5 Place the baking tray on the middle shelf of the preheated oven and bake the pies for about 15 minutes, or until the pastry turns golden and the mincemeat starts to boil slightly. Remove from the oven and allow to cool slightly before taking the pies out of their tin.

6 Sprinkle the mince pies with icing sugar and serve immediately. To add a festive feel, the mince pie tops could be shaped with a star cutter or perhaps a holly-shaped cutter.

Bûche de Noël

This is a very special addition to any tea table, and a wonderful way
to celebrate Christmas.

For the chocolate meringue sponge:
3 free-range eggs, separated
50g (¼ cup) unrefined caster sugar
20g (¼ cup) cocoa powder, sieved

For the pistachio crème brûlée:
4 free-range egg yolks
1 free-range egg
100g (½ cup) unrefined caster sugar
500ml (2 cups) double cream
15g (1 tablespoon) pistachio paste

For the chocolate mousse:
250g (9oz) dark chocolate (minimum
65% cocoa solids)
100ml (⅜ cup) whole milk
250ml (1 cup) whipping cream
4.5 free-range egg yolks
45g (¼ cup) golden caster sugar
25g (⅛ cup) unsalted butter, diced and
softened

For the chocolate ganache:
350ml (1½ cups) whipping cream
350g (12oz) dark chocolate (54% cocoa
solids), broken up

Plus: 120g (4oz) drained Griottine
cherries (cherries preserved in brandy)

To make the chocolate meringue sponge:

1 Preheat the oven to 170ºC (325ºF, gas mark 3).

2 Whisk the egg whites and gradually add the caster sugar to form a stiff meringue base. Fold through the egg yolks and then the sieved cocoa powder. Grease and line a flat Swiss roll tin with baking paper and then carefully and evenly spread the meringue mixture on to the tray.

3 Place in the oven and bake until the sponge springs back to shape when pressed with your finger. Times will vary depending upon your type of oven, but allow about 8 minutes. Once baked, immediately turn the meringue sponge on to another sheet of baking paper and allow to cool. Trim to a 25 × 7 cm rectangle, and set to one side until needed.

To make the pistachio crème brûlée:

4 Preheat the oven to 130°C (250°F, gas mark ½).

5 Place the cream and pistachio paste into a saucepan and bring almost to the boil. Whisk the eggs and sugar together, and gradually pour the almost-boiling cream onto the whisking eggs. Pass the mixture through a sieve and pour into the rectangular silicone mould. Place in a bain marie on the middle shelf of the preheated oven. Cook until set.

6 Remove the crème from the oven and chill down completely before placing in a freezer to firm. Once firm, remove from the silicone mould.

recipe continued overleaf

Bûche de Noël *continued*

Equipment:
26 cm/10" Bûche de Noël metal
mould, rectangular heat-proof silicone
baking tray or mould 26 × 3 cm/10
× 1.25" (or thereabouts), fine sieve or
muslin cloth

To make the chocolate mousse:

7 Semi-whip the cream. Whisk together the egg yolks and sugar. Boil the milk, and once boiled pour on to the whisked egg yolks. Return to the saucepan and cook slowly until it starts to thicken. As soon as it does, immediately remove from the heat and pour through a fine sieve or a muslin cloth on to the dark chocolate. Stir until all of the chocolate has melted and the mix is smooth. The chocolate mix should cool slightly before carefully folding through the whipped cream.

To make the chocolate ganache:

8 Boil the cream and then pour on to the chocolate, whisking until smooth.

To assemble:

9 Line the Bûche de Noël mould carefully with cling film. Pipe chocolate mousse into the mould up to just below halfway. Tap the mould to remove any air bubbles. Carefully place the crème brûlée insert on to the mousse, arranging drained Griottine cherries on either side. Pipe the rest of the mousse into the mould until just below the top and smooth with a palette knife. Place the prepared chocolate meringue sponge rectangle on top and again tap gently. Place in the fridge to set, until the bûche is firm enough to be able to remove from the mould.

10 Once demoulded, place on a wire rack and pour the chocolate ganache over, making sure that the chocolate mousse is completely covered without any gaps. Allow to set before placing on a serving plate and decorating as required.

UK and US Weights and Measures

Oven temperatures

°C	°F	Gas mark
110	225	1/4
130	250	1/2
140	275	1
150	300	2
170	325	3
180	350	4
190	375	5
200	400	6
220	425	7
230	450	8
240	475	9

American weights and measures

Guide to conversions

	Metric	Imperial	US
Flour/Cocoa	25g	1oz	1/4 cup
	50g	2oz	1/2 cup
	75g	3oz	3/4 cup
	100g	4oz	1 cup
	120g	4 1/2 oz	1 cup
Butter/Sugar	25g	1oz	2 tbsp
	50g	2oz	1/4 cup
	100g	4oz	1/2 cup
	175g	6oz	3/4 cup
	225g	8oz	1 cup
Grated cheese	100g	4 oz	1 cup

Cake Tin Sizing Chart

15cm	6 inch
18cm	7 inch
20cm	8 inch
23cm	9 inch
25cm	10 inch

All eggs are size large unless otherwise stated.

ACKNOWLEDGMENTS

We are grateful to Her Majesty The Queen for permission to produce this book.

Amongst those who have given invaluable assistance in its creation: all the kitchen team but particularly Mark Fromont, Giuliano Vilardo, Tim Doncaster, Victoria Scupham and James Bointon. Grateful thanks also to Stephen Murray, Yeoman of the Silver and Gilt Pantry, and to Stephen Marshall, Yeoman of the Glass Pantry. We are also most grateful to Peter Whorton, Darryl Newman, Philip Rhodes and all the Footmen and Pages; and to Richard Thompson, David Rough and team.

Thanks also to Colonel Duncan Dewar, Windsor Castle Superintendent; to Lorraine Dale, Rachel Gordon and all the team at Windsor Castle, and particularly to Admiral Sir James Perowne, The Constable and Governor of the Castle.

Finally we would like to thank Cynthia Inions and Lisa Linder for the superb photography; Lucy Gowans for her design; Nina Chang for testing and editing the recipes; and the Royal Collection Publications team of Jacky Colliss Harvey, David Tibbs and Debbie Wayment.

Published 2017 by Royal Collection Trust

York House
St James's Palace
London SW1A 1BQ

**Explore the Royal Collection at
www.royalcollection.org.uk**

ISBN 978 1 909741 33 1

101058

British Library Cataloguing in Publication data:
A catalogue record of this book is available from
the British Library.

Photography by **Lisa Linder**
Styling by **Cynthia Inions**
Designed by **Lucy Gowans**
Production Manager **Debbie Wayment**

Typeset in Berthold Baskerville and Revista
Printed on Gardmat 150gsm
Colour reproduction by Tag Publishing
Printed and bound in Slovenia by Gorenjski tisk